OSVALDO GOLIJOV
LÚA DESCOLORIDA

FOR ONE STRING INSTRUMENT AND PIANO

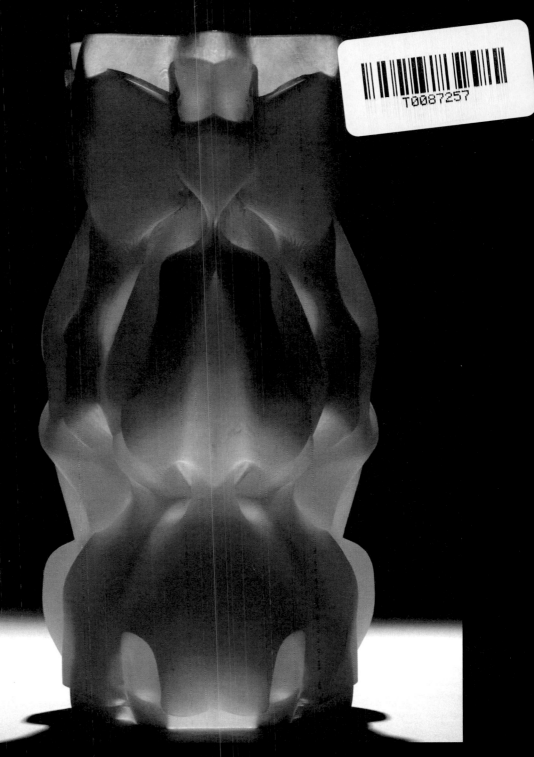

HENDON MUSIC

BOOSEY & HAWKES

AN IMAGEM COMPANY

DISTRIBUTED BY

HAL•LEONARD®
CORPORATION
7777 W. BLUEMOUND RD. P.O. BOX 13819 MILWAUKEE, WI 53213

www.boosey.com

www.halleonard.com

Published by Hendon Music, Inc.
a Boosey & Hawkes company
229 West 28th Street, 11th Floor
New York NY 10001

www.boosey.com

ISMN 979-0-051-10639-4

Cover art by Neri Oxman. Used by permission.

Printed in U.S.A. and distributed by Hal Leonard Corporation, Milwaukee WI
First Printing, 2011
Music typesetting by Arturo Rodriguez

Originally scored for Soprano and Piano,
this work was commissioned by the Barlow Endowment for Music Composition
Brigham Young University

Duration: ca. 6'

COMPOSER'S NOTES

"A dead man in Spain is more alive than anywhere else," said García Lorca, explaining that Spanish poets define rather than allude. *Lúa Descolorida*, a poem written in Gallego (the language of the Galicia region in Spain) by Lorca's beloved Rosalía de Castro, defines despair in a way that is simultaneously tender and tragic. The musical setting is a constellation of clearly defined symbols that affirm contradictory things at the same time, becoming in the end a suspended question mark. The song is at once a slow motion ride on a cosmic horse, a homage to Couperin's melismas in his *Lessons of Tenebrae*, velvet bells coming from three different churches, heaven as seen once by Yeats, a death lullaby, and the ladder of Jacob's dream. But the strongest inspiration for *Lúa Descolorida* was Dawn Upshaw's rainbow of a voice, and I wanted to give her a piece so radiant that it would bring an echo of the single tear that Schubert brings without warning in his voicing of a G major chord. There are two versions of the song with soprano soloist, written for specific musicians: one for Gil Kalish's pearl piano playing, the other for the "early morning bows" of the Kronos Quartet. One other version exists, for soprano and string orchestra.

—*Osvaldo Golijov*

NOTAS DE LA MÚSICA

"Un muerto en España está más vivo como muerto que en ningún sitio del mundo," dijo García Lorca, explicando que los poetas españoles definen en vez de aludir. Lúa Descolorida, un poema escrito en gallego de Rosalía de Castro que era tan querida por Lorca, define la desesperación de una manera simultáneamente tierna y trágica. El contexto musical es una constelación de símbolos claramente definidos que afirman cosas contradictorias al mismo tiempo, convirtiéndose al final en un signo de pregunta suspendido. La canción es a su vez un viaje a cámara lenta en un caballo cósmico, un homenaje a las melismas de Couperin en sus Lecciones de Tinieblas, campanas de terciopelo que repican desde tres iglesias diferentes, el cielo como lo viera alguna vez Yeats, un lamento fúnebre y la escalera del sueño de Jacob. Pero la inspiración más fuerte de Lúa Descolorida fue el arco iris de voz de Dawn Upshaw y le quise regalar una pieza tan radiante que trajera un eco de la lágrima solitaria que brinda sin aviso Schubert al armonizar un acorde de sol mayor. Hay dos versiones de la canción compuesta para músicos específicos con una solista soprano: una es para la perla del piano de Gil Kalish y la otra para "los arcos mañaneros" del Kronos Quartet. También existe una version más, para soprano y orquesta de cuerdas."

—*Osvaldo Golijov*

ANMERKUNGEN
DES KOMPONISTEN

"Ein toter Mann ist lebendiger in Spanien als irgend anderswo", sagte García Lorca erklärend, dass spanische Dichter eher Grenzen definieren anstatt zu berühren. *Lua Descolorida*, ein Gedicht in Gallego (die Sprache der in Spanien gelegenen Region Galizien) von Lorca's geliebter Rosalía de Castro geschrieben, definiert Verzweiflung in einer Weise, die ebenso zart wie tragisch ist. Die musikalische Inszenierung ist eine Konstellation von klar definierten Symbolen, die zugleich widersprüchliche Dinge behaupten und sich gegen Ende als Fragezeichen wiederspiegeln. Das Lied ist auf einmal ein zeitlupen Ritt auf einem kosmischen Pferd, eine Hommage an Couperin Melismen in seinen *Lessons of Tenebrae*, drei von verschiedenen Kirchen läutenden samtigen Glocken, Himmel wie einst von Yeats gesehen, ein Todeswiegenlied und Jakob's Traumleiter. Jedoch war die grösste Inspiration für *Lua Descolorida* Dawn Upshaw's Regenbogen einer Stimme. Ich wollte ihr ein so strahlendes Stück überbringen, dass es ein Echo jeder einzelnen Träne sei, die Schubert ohne Vorwarnung durch sein Voicing eines einzelnen G-dur-Akkords hervorruft. Es gibt zwei Versionen diesem Lieder für Sopransolistin, geschrieben für besondere Musiker: eine für Gil Kalish's perlendes Klavierspiel, die andere für die "frühmorgen" Streicher des Kronosquartets. Zusätzlich zu der vorliegenden Ausgabe existiert eine weitere Version für Sopran und Streichorchester.

—*Osvaldo Golijov*

TEXT

Lua Descolorida

by Rosalía de Castro

Lúa descolorida
como cor de ouro pálido,
vesme i eu non quixera
me vises de tan alto.
Ó espaso que recorres,
lévame, caladiña, nun teu raio.

Astro das almas orfas,
lúa descolorida,
eu ben sei que n'alumas
tristeza cal a miña.
Vai contalo ó teu dono,
e dille que me leve adonde habita.

Mais non lle contes nada,
descolorida lúa,
pois nin neste nin noutros
mundos teréis fertuna.
Se sabes onde a morte
ten a morada escura,
dille que corpo e alma xuntamente
me leve adonde non recorden nunca,
nin no mundo en que estóu nin nas alturas.

Colorless Moon

by Rosalía de Castro

Moon, colorless
like the color of pale gold:
You see me here and I wouldn't like you
to see me from the heights above.
Take me, silently, in your ray
to the space of your journey.

Star of the orphan souls,
Moon, colorless:
I know that you don't illuminate
sadness as sad as mine.
Go and tell it to your master
and tell him to take me to his place.

But don't tell him anything,
Moon, colorless,
because my fate won't change
here or in other worlds.
If you know where Death
has her dark mansion,
Tell her to take my body and soul together
To a place where I won't be remembered,
Neither in this world, nor in the heights above.

LÚA DESCOLORIDA

for One String Instrument and Piano

OSVALDO GOLIJOV

979-0-051-10639-4

STRING PART

LÚA DESCOLORIDA
for One String Instrument and Piano

OSVALDO GOLIJOV

liquid, sweet

4

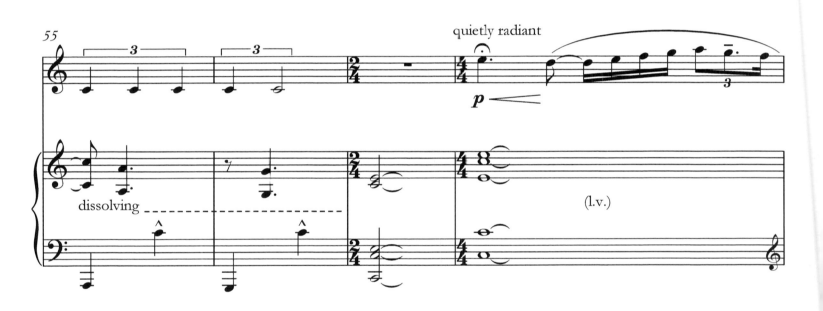